TECHNIQUES O

THE ESSENCE OF

Hakkoryu Jujutsu

Dennis G. Palumbo
KAIDEN SHIHAN SAN DAI KICHU

Other books by Dennis G. Palumbo:

The Secrets of Hakkoryu Jujutsu: Shodan Tactics

Secret Nidan Techniques of Hakkoryu Jujutsu

The Essence of Hakkoryu Jujutsu:
Techniques of Sandan Gi
by Dennis G. Palumbo

Copyright © 1993 by Dennis G. Palumbo

ISBN 0-87364-860-9
Printed in the United States of America

Published by Paladin Press, a division of
Paladin Enterprises, Inc., P.O. Box 1307,
Boulder, Colorado 80306, USA.
(303) 443-7250

Direct inquiries and/or orders to the above address.

Table of Contents

To Nidai Soke Okuyama and Kaiden Shihan Murakami.
To my teachers past and present; my students;
my family: Dora, Debbie, Denise, Stephanie, and Vincent.
To all current and future practitioners
of the art of Hakkoryu: may this in some way
help you along the way.

Dennis G. Palumbo
Kaiden Shihan San Dai Kichu

Mr. Dennis G. Palumbo, Kaiden Shihan San Dai Kichu, is the Founder and the Director of Hakkoryu Martial Arts Federation (HMAF), and the SHIDO (Defensive Initiative Tactics Institute (DITI), as well as the Personal Empowerment Program (PEP), a Full Force Self Protection Program for Women. Mr. Palumbo began his formal studies of the martial arts in 1958 in Yanagi Ryu, Aiki Jujutsu, in his home town of Lynwood, California. Upon entering the Air Force he continued, studying Karate in Texas. His first assignment was overseas to Japan where he began his study of Hakkoryu Jujutsu, with Shihan Hideo B. Abukawa - eventually attaining the rank of Shihan, in November 1963, making him only the 5th American to be awarded this title.

Returning to the U.S. in 1964, he earned his Shodan in Shotokan Karate in 1965, and began teaching Hakkoryu Jujutsu in Texas. He returned to Japan in 1966, and remained until 1970 teaching Hakkoryu and studying Shotokan, Shudokan, and Goju Ryu Karate. Returning to the states in 1970, he studied and taught at the University of Colorado and also studied Shito Ryu Karate for 11/2 years. In 1970 he was asked to return to Japan by Soke Okuyama, but was unable to attend because of Air Force duties. In 1972 he was assigned to duty in Fairbanks, Alaska and also won his promotion to Sandan in Shotokan Karate. He formed the HMAF in San Angelo, Texas in 1974. It has been operating successfully and is recognized internationally as a premier legitimate organization fostering the martial arts tradition. In June of 1980 Mr. Palumbo returned to Japan for a month to undergo training and testing by Soke Okuyama. He was awarded the titles and ranks of Renshi, and then Menkyo Kaiden. In the summer of 1986, he was awarded the title of SAN DAI KICHU, the highest possible ranking in Hakkoryu Jujutsu.

Mr. Palumbo has had extensive experience teaching and training not only members of the U.S. Military, but also the Ohio State Patrol, Denver Police Dept., Aurora Police Dept., members of the OSI, Air Force Security Police, FBI, Colorado Bureau of Investigation (CBI), and the United States Treasury Department. He was awarded the rank of Honorary Lieutenant by the Chief of the Denver Police Department in 1988.

Mr. Palumbo holds a Bachelor of Science Degree in Transportation and Manpower Management from the University of Colorado, a Master of Arts (MA) in Psychology

Counseling and Guidance from the University of Northern Colorado, and is currently a PhD. candidate in Criminal Justice Management. He has written numerous articles for martial arts magazines, handicapped magazines, and produced video tapes as well as having three books on Hakkoryu Jujutsu published. He is a certified advanced practitioner and lecturer of Koho Shiatsu, and the Police PR-24 baton.

Mr. Palumbo currently holds the following ranks and titles:

RANK	MARTIAL ART
Kaiden Shihan San Dai Kichu	Hakkoryu Jujutsu
Yondan (4th Degree Black Belt)	Shotokan Karate
Yondan (4th Degree Black Belt)	Taiho-Jutsu (Arrest and Control Tactics)
Nidan (2nd Degree Black Belt)	Goju-Ryu Karate
Shodan (lst Degree Black Belt)	Shudokan Karate

DIRECTOR:	Hakkoryu Martial Arts Federation (HMAF)
SHIDO:	Defensive-Initiative Tactics Institute (DITI)
SHIDO:	Japanese Shiatsu Massage Institute
CHIEF INSTRUCTOR:	National Peace Officer Defensive Tactics Instructors Association
MEMBER:	Board of Review and Selection: Who's Who in the Martial Arts.
INSTRUCTOR:	Red Rocks Community College (Colorado) Dept. of Criminal Justice - Police Tactics

AFFILIATIONS

The HMAF is recognized by, and closely affiliated with the following organizations:

HAKKORYU SO-HOMBU, ZENKOKU SHIHANKAI - Omiya, Japan
American Jujitsu Association (AJA)
American Judo & Jujitsu Federation (AJJF)
Society of Black Belts (U.K.)
World Tai Jutsu Federation (U.K.)
    European Jujitsu Union World Butokukai Headquarters (U.K. & Japan)
    American-Japan Karate Association (USA) (AJKA)
USAKF (U.S. AM. KARATE FED.)

Introduction

I am very pleased to present to you for the first time, this third book in the series on HAKKORYU JUJUTSU. This book on the techniques of Sandan Waza will round out your knowledge and understanding of this most effective and interesting Martial Art. This book is the logical and systematic follow-up to my first two books: The Secret Shodan Tactics of Hakkoryu Jujutsu, and Nidan Tactics of Hakkoryu Jujutsu. With the basic ground work laid in the first two books, you will be able to progress in your understanding and application of Hakkoryu waza and principles to the level of an accomplished practitioner. You will be introduced to the extremely effective and painful *GAKUN* grip, the painful and controlling technique of *Mochi Maware*, and various training techniques to build your grip and strengthen your arms.

You will be introduced to three major pressure point meridians and their immediate and long range effects on the body. This will be extremely useful in controlling an adversary. Through diligent study and practice, your mastery of the Waza of Sandan Gi will provide you with a multitude of options for personal defense and healthy practice. You will also be introduced to some simple yet effective acupressure (Shiatsu) massage techniques to help relieve tension and stiffness in the joints.

I wish you the best in your studies with this book and continued success in your mastery of the principles of Hakkoryu Jujutsu.

DENNIS G. "KEMPO" PALUMBO
Kaiden Shihan San Dai Kichu

❖ *Chapter One* ❖

Theory of Training for SANDAN GI of Hakkoryu

As you will see in your reading of this third book in the series on Hakkoryu Jujutsu, the waza of Sandan Gi are related in many ways to the Waza of Nidan. Many of the techniques have the same name, but are performed in a different manner, involving a special lock unique to Hakkoryu. This finishing lock-up is utilized in several of the Sandan Waza, and can be very painful at first. Therefore you will be shown some exercises later in the section on Methods of Training to stretch certain muscles in the arm and upper body so as to minimize discomfort in training, and improve your overall flexibility. As the Soke of Hakkoryu says, when training in the techniques of Sandan Gi, it is "... extremely important to use no strength, make the heart light, and the chest empty." This is much easier said than done! However, relaxation again becomes the key to successful application of the techniques of Sandan Gi.

You will soon realize that if strength is applied by the Tori, it actually negates the extremely painful and effective grip of the Gakun. The application of Atemi (strike or pressure to a vital point on the body) becomes a matter of accuracy rather than power. In fact, the use of power will subvert your attempt to make this powerful grip work successfully. Principles learned earlier in Shodan and Nidan, such as Te Kagami (Hand Mirror) and Maki Komi (Wrapping Technique) will be applied during this course of Sandan Gi in a slightly different manner. The dynamic principle of Mochi Maware (to lead around and lift up) will be demonstrated as part of the Sandan Waza. You will see how this principle, combined with that of the Gakun, will allow you to lead an adversary to any position or place you desire; permitting you to finally pin, restrain, or throw him, if that is your desire.

An aspect of training which you must adhere to, especially in the practice

Techniques of Sandan Gi: The Essence of Hakkoryu Jujutsu

of Sandan Gi is the amount of time you devote to application of certain techniques such as the Gakun. In Sandan, the application of the Gakun (effective grip) to a meridian of the body known in Japanese as the "Dai Cho Kei" (large intestine meridian), could leave one with some unexpected "side effects."

I recall my first unexpected experience with these "side effects" while training in Wakkanai, Japan with my Sensei, Abukawa Shihan. During my last year in Wakkanai, I practiced with him daily in an attempt to progress to the point of qualifying to train for Shihan. We practiced with much vigor and energy. I gradually became quite accustomed to the pain of Shodan Waza, and quite resilient in accepting the continual sharp pain of Nidan Waza. My wrists had grown considerably over the months of training, and felt quite invulnerable to most types of attack, twists, binds, etc. I affectionately came to refer to my Sensei as "The Man with the Iron Wrists" because his wrists were close to 13 inches in circumference while his stature was only 5' 2". He introduced me to the Sandan grip named GAKUN . As we practiced, I applied the Gakun on him and began to see results. He, in turn, would continually perform the technique on me to give me the "true" meaning of the techniques.

Our practice would sometimes last 2 to 2l/2 hours, solely on the waza of Sandan technique, after which we would shower and go to the Airmen's club for something to eat and a couple of cold Sapporo beers. Inevitably, a few hours after practice I would come down with tremendous gas pains in my lower stomach. I initially attributed these pains to the food which was served at the Airmen's club (it wasn't exactly known for its "haute cuisine"); it was as if I'd eaten spoiled food. After an hour or so of suffering these "disparisms: (as they were called in the Airborne program), I would invariably have to relieve myself. This unpleasant situation of relieving oneself was sometimes colorfully described in GI terms as "Montezuma's Revenge" or "The Green Apple Quick Step". In any event I am sure you can picture this "side effect" which can be a result of extended practice of the Gakun grip.

My evaluation to be allowed to test for Shihan eventually arrived. I was to travel to the Hombu for Hakkoryu in Tokyo, Japan. I became accustomed to these "disparisms" as a result of training and mistakenly thought the change in food and culture at the Hombu would not cause this unpleasant feeling. During the second day of training however, after working extensively on the techniques of Sandan, the same unpleasant feelings struck again. I forgot to bring Kaopectate or Pepto-Bismol to help me through this discomfort and finally asked my Sensei what to do.

He said, "Weren't you practicing Sandan Gi in the dojo this afternoon?"

I replied affirmatively. He laughed and continued, "...I guess I should have told you that extensive practice of the Gakun will give you the GI's."

"You've got to be kidding me!", I stated. "You mean to tell me that after all these months, the reason I've been having these reactions after practice is because of the Gakun?"

"Oh yes", he countered, "that particular meridian is the Dai Cho Kei, or large intestine meridian. Among other things, it is used to clear up irregularity." He paused, then continued. "Of course if you haven't figured it out by now, you will learn more about this during Shihan training."

Well it was easy to see how this became the standard joke of the resident Shihans during my stay at the Hombu. After meals, one of them would always confront me, jokingly grab my wrist and push on the point of the Dai Cho Kei meridian, and saying something like "...this will help you get ready for your next meal!" Ha! Ha!

The training in Sandan waza will at first place some strain on the anterior deltoid muscles of the arm. This muscle comes into play quite often since many of the waza finish in a unique lock. The Sandan lock is used extensively in this level and, at first, those individuals who are well developed, such as body builders and weight lifters, are very stiff or do not have sufficient elasticity in their shoulders and deltoid muscles, will experience some severe pain.

The theory of training in Sandan Gi goes beyond that explained in Volume II of this series: *The Secret Nidan Techniques of Hakkoryu Jujutsu.*

Soke Okayama has stated "The Sandan (3rd degree black belt) in Hakkoryu, is most assuredly capable of confronting several adversaries concurrently. He now executes his techniques with properly applied power, more speed and precision. His knowledge of the various meridians of the body and their effect on certain internal organs, provides him another dimension in his response to attack. This is the level of which a practitioner has become more than just a technician."

Evaluation for advancement to this level includes a complete review of all prior levels of accomplishment making sure all waza are correctly performed and the underlying principles understood. The student's ability must demonstrate an easy transition from one level to the next in the application of technique. The Sandan's abilities must include an ability to shift from one technique to another, without hesitation, should one technique fail or be countered. At the request of the instructor, he or she must also be able to demonstrate multiple applications of a technique and/or principle. Alternatively, the Sandan may also be requested to demonstrate the application of multiple principles from various levels within the application of a single technique. These multiple principles might include a principle from Shodan, then Sandan, finishing with a Nidan technique or principle in the course of one application. Additionally, the student might be required to demonstrate a basic principle (such as Gakun) from an unusual type of attack (such as the headlock). The ability of the student to do this in the presence of the instructor with little or no hesitation reinforces the students readiness for advancement.

Simultaneously during the training period prior to testing, the student is closely evaluated for his or her contributions to the dojo, the other students, classes, Sensei, and Hakkoryu. Throughout this training period the following items are just a few considered during the evaluation for advancement, Does the new candidate have the ability to teach and correct mistakes made by new or lower ranking students during class? Can the candidate spot mistakes and explain to the student the principle involved in addition to the repercussions of such an error? When asked, does the new candidate have the ability to conduct class properly and respond to queries posed him by the students? Has the candidate recognized when the Kohai (Junior students) are fulfilling their duties to the dojo, in such areas as cleanliness, respect, attention, attendance, paying of fees, and performing the myriad of things required in a dojo to keep it clean and honorable? Is he or she a good example of what the Sensei represents?

The concept of self defense in Hakkoryu was treated at some length in Volume II of this series. However, the area of Atemi waza as used in Nidan, is slightly different in Sandan. The primary attention to Atemi waza was devoted to striking certain vulnerable vital points in the body. In Sandan, the application of Atemi involves more of the pressing of certain points on the body, through the use of the Gakun grip. For basic waza these virtually stop the flow of energy (KI) at each point. There are more applications on other parts of the body, as will be illustrated, using these same principles which can cause excruciating pain, and drop a person in their tracks. Great care must be taken in the use of the Gakun grip, lest you inflict such severe pain on your practice partner inadvertently. The Gakun grip can be so powerful that, if used improperly, it is actually possible to fracture a person's ulnar bone. Exercise care in these techniques!

In learning the waza of Sandan Gi, you will perfect additional responses to:

- ❈ attacks to the front of the body.
- ❈ grabs on the arm.
- ❈ pulls from the side.
- ❈ chokes from the rear applied along with armbar.
- ❈ defense against grabs on the shoulders (epaulet) from the front and the rear.
- ❈ bear hugs from the rear.
- ❈ rear double arm grabs.
- ❈ overhand strikes.
- ❈ straight punches to the body.
- ❈ grabs on the belt from both the front and the rear.
- ❈ defense against one who is drawing a sword, or thrusting with a knife or a dagger.

Additionally, as was illustrated in the previous two volumes, a series of walking exercises designed to defend against weapons attacks from the rear, kick defenses, and up close attacks will be presented. The Tori's (defender) ability to give way at the right instant, and move his body correctly (Tai Sabaki) becomes extremely important when dealing with defenses against the sword and the knife. Since defenses at this level against such attacks involve exact and immediate application of the Gakun grip, your practice must bring you to the point where you can apply the grip to the proper point immediately and without hesitation. Remember, there is only a split second between life, which is short, and death, which is long. Attempt to keep this in mind when practicing and apply as much realism as you can to your training. Do not practice the techniques lazily or haphazardly; only half finishing them either because you believe "you've got it down"' or maybe because your Kake (attacker) is a little tired or sore. If the Kake is too sore to continue, proceed to less painful techniques or practice with another Kake.

Practice diligently! Expend all your effort (Doryoku)! Maintain an energetic mental attitude (Konjyo), while tempering your actions and training with mercy (Jihi). The effectiveness of each of the four major principles of Sandan Gi (Gakun, Mochi Maware, Te Kagami, and Maki Komi) depends on precision, speed, surprise, and **practice.**

Training Point To Help In Your Progress

As mentioned earlier, certain muscles of the shoulder may require a bit more range of flexibility to allow you to learn these techniques, and thereby allow your partner to perform them without causing you undue pain. At this point, if someone should get you into such a position, you would be able to endure a considerably greater amount of pressure than if your upper body muscles - especially the shoulders - were tight. After practicing the techniques of Sandan, you may also experience some discomfort in your body and arms. I will, therefore, give some examples of how to relieve this discomfort. I will give you suggestions on how to condition your forearms to take the strain of Sandan training, and how to develop a powerful grip, through the exercises of Gakun.

With these suggestions you may well discover other exercises that are just as useful in your training. Emphasis must be placed on devoting time before, after, and between workouts to develop these exercises, your arms, and your shoulders.

I. Exercise to strengthen and lengthen the anterior deltoid muscle range. Using your belt or a towel, grip the belt with one hand; the other hand should grip the opposite end of the belt. Place the first behind your back, at about waist level. Relax your breathing, and as you begin to slowly exhale, pull upward with the free hand on the belt, lifting your hand as high as possible, toward your shoulder blade. You must relax while performing this exercise or you will strain the muscles in your shoulder causing them to spasm and tighten up. Gradually pull up on the hand as high as you can and hold this position for 10 seconds or as long as possible.

Relax the tension and as you begin to lower the hand to your waist, resist slightly with the pulling hand. Switch positions and start over. Complete this exercise at least 6 times daily to increase the range and strength of your anterior deltoid muscle. (Photos A & B)

A

B

II. Developing strength of the grip. The point at the base of your index finger is the main point of pressure for application of the Gakun grip atemi mentioned earlier. To develop this point on your finger and thereby the power of the Gakun grip, a person can practice with a broom handle or the steering wheel of your car. (Photo C) Another helpful method is to practice the grip on yourself. This has two effects: 1) It helps to practice the grip properly, making sure your hand is in the proper place on the wrist each time, and 2) it begins to desensitize your own wrists to the Gakun which others may apply to you. Desensitizing may take some time to accomplish. (Photo D)

C

D

III. Wrist flexibility and strength. Using a short stick (12-24 inches), grip the stick firmly with one hand, rotate the stick outward from your body in the full range of motion of the gripping wrist, hold for 10-15 seconds or as long as possible, at this extreme point. Next, reversing your free hand grip, turn the wrist in the opposite direction with the arm extended to the front, to the extreme limit of the wrist's range. Again, hold this position 10-15 seconds, or as long as possible. It is important to keep the tension and to not let the grip loosen on the hand being rotated, especially with the last two or three fingers. (Photo E)

E

IV. After Practice Conditioning. Before and after a vigorous practice of Nidan and Sandan Gi Waza, it is very helpful to perform a stretching and muscle relaxing exercise with your partner. Gripping his forearm with one hand, and his hand with the other, bend the wrist and, while turning his hand in one direction, turn the forearm in the opposite direction - slowly, gradually increasing the range of flexibility. Do four or five repetitions of this motion on each arm, before and after practice. This will help to desensitize the wrists and forearms for the strain of Nidan and Sandan techniques. (Photos F&G)

F

G

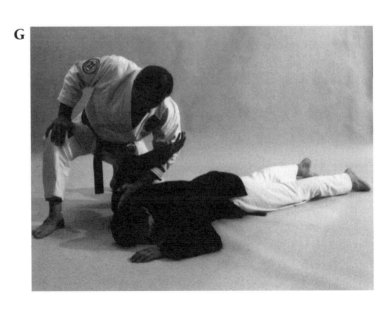

Benefits And Applications Of Sandan Gi Waza

Aside from learning advanced applications of Sandan waza, you will become acquainted with the important meridian lines of the Large Intestine and the Small Intestine. These meridians are located on the inside radial and ulnar outside surfaces of the top of the forearm. These two meridians are used quite extensively in the execution of the Sandan waza. At first these areas are quite sensitive to the application of pressure from the Gakun grip, but over a period of time the pain of a properly applied grip will have little effect on the receiver. Additionally, you will learn more sophisticated waza utilizing the painful and restricting arm lock of Sandan Gi, and Gakun, dealing with attacks or grabs from the front; the humbling lock and pin of Sandan Te Kagami; using the powerful Gakun grip as a defense from front punch and overhand strike; defenses for a strike from the side by being pulled or grabbed; defense against a rear grab and choke, applied with an armbar; the powerful unbalancing and controlling principle of Mochi Maware; using Tai Sabaki and the Gakun grip as defenses against the drawing of a tanto (knife) and/or katana (sword); the double Gakun application of Riote Mochi Maware which allows you to throw and pin your attacker, pinning both of his arms, thereby placing him in a painful and totally immobile position; defenses against pickpockets from the rear, including belt grabs, from both the front and the rear; defenses for use against the ever popular rear bear hug, shoulder grabs from both the front and the rear, and two hand rear attacks.

With the inclusion of eight added walking exercises designed especially for this level of training, you will learn defenses against rear attacks with a gun or knife; front kick defensive options; two more up close grabs or strikes defenses, defense against rear weapon attack with a stick or a longer weapon, surprise rear two handed grab or attack, and up-close groin kick defense. Finally this book includes some basic Shiatsu (finger pressure) treatments for relief of stiffness, sore muscles, and body relaxation to be performed after workouts or whenever you feel a need for a good physical uplift.

The "Tekiyo" of Hakkoryu Jujutsu

It may seem to the casual or uninitiated observer that many of the techniques or "waza" do not have specific relevance to self-defense situations because of the way in which Hakkoryu Jujutsu is taught, learned, and practiced. At first glance this is expected and understandable. However, the essence of Hakkoryu lies beyond the more obvious learning of its waza and must be reached through continual practice to allow the development of its "Tekiyo" (applications).

Tekiyo are different than "Henka" (variations) in several respects. Tekiyo, or application, is a consideration that every student is concerned about from the beginning of their training. This is understandable and should be expected by the instructor. Why else would a person undertake the study of a "self-defense" art, if not to understand or learn its application? Henka, variation, is normally referred to as "a change to" or variation. For example, the changing of the ending of a particular waza from possibly a pin control to an "atemi" strike as the finish. This is considered to be a "basic" variation by many practitioners of Hakkoryu. The Henka is normally allowed only after a student has mastered the basic waza of a specific level and is working toward the mastering of waza of the next level, i.e. SHODAN Gi waza to the NIDAN or SANDAN waza. The use of Henka by beginning students is strongly discouraged by the instructor since a student who has not fully mastered the basic techniques of a particular level can easily confuse an ending of basic variation with the original or, as Soke Okuyama refers to it, "true" ending of the technique. The student is reminded not to be too concerned about learning or practicing Henka at too early a stage in his training. There is always plenty of time to practice and develop Henka by the practitioner as he or she progresses in their training.

As mentioned before, one of the primary areas of emphasis in Hakkoryu Jujutsu is the understanding and mastery of specific principles related to the various levels of accomplishment. Without completely understanding and mastering these principles through repeated training in waza, the student can never successfully proceed to apply Henka let alone the more important aspect of Tekiyo. This is the ultimate goal or purpose of any art of personal self-defense. Unlike various arts designed more specifically for "sport" competition, a self-defense art should not be overly concerned about competitive application. For example, the main concern of a Bujutsu or Bugei (art) is its relevance to the situation at hand, and the application of its principles to a self-defense situation; whatever it may be. A student of Hakkoryu must therefore continually strive to master the basic waza so as to be able to perform them at any time, on any person, in any situation one might encounter. This is indeed a monumental training goal in any art that is not sport competition oriented.

In the dojo (training hall) we can only practice what "might" happen in

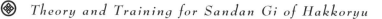

self defense situations with as much realism as the instructor allows so as to prevent serious injury. During these periods of training the student must have in mind that each situation, no matter how simplistic or seemingly unreal, is being studied for a purpose, i.e. its possible application at a later date, or in a different situation.

Without this the student will be merely "going through the motions" of training. Consequently, when the time should come for real application of his technique he will fail in his efforts to thwart the threat to his person.

In a Hakkoryu dojo, students continually practice with different students. The Sempai/Kohai (Senior/Junior) student relationship is very important. The Sempai is responsible for implementing the correct transmission of waza and making sure the student thoroughly understands the principle (Gokui) of a speciflc waza. After a period of time training with his or her Sempai, the junior student rotates to train with other students of a higher or lower rank. During rotation the student begins to realize that a speciflc technique which might have worked well on one student might not work as easily on another, more advanced student. An attempt is thereby made to practice and be able to make that technique work as easily on the advanced student as it might have earlier on a junior student. Through this continual rotation and practice the student gradually perfects his techniques.

✦ *Chapter Two* ✦

The Journey Towards Mastery

People who take up a martial art for the first time do so for varying reasons. Some to develop their self confidence; some to feel better about themselves; some to prove something to themselves or others and; some just for the enjoyment of training. In his article for Esquire Magazine, Mr. George Leonard discusses the subject of "Mastery" of a sport, or any endeavor for that matter.[1] He explains the "ups and downs" a person might encounter on the road to mastery. In terms of a learning curve, examples are given to illustrate the curve of the "Dabbler", the "Obsessive", and the "Hacker" along with that of the mastery curve.

The study of martial art falls perfectly into these categories defined by Mr. Leonard. Since "Mastery" is such an overused, yet rarely attained term in the martial arts, some thought should be given by the new student as to his or her attitude in this light. The elusive category of master is not a goal easily attained, if ever. In fact, the true master rarely considers him or herself to be just that, i.e. a true master. He is content to continue striving, recognizing the plateaus that are inevitable, looking forward to the growth that will eventually come, and minimizing the length of time on each plateau.

As an instructor of the martial arts and practitioner for more than 30 years, the characteristics of the "Dabbler" are one of the most easily recognizable of the categories which is addressed by Mr. Leonard. He is the new, super enthusiastic student who is so excited about the new endeavor he just can't keep it to himself. He tells everyone, wife, girlfriend, co-workers, friends, who ever will listen, about his new adventure. The "Dabbler" talks of the new uniform, the discipline, the courtesies he is learning, the new techniques, etc; his immediate progress recharges his enthusiasm. However, he soon reaches his first plateau. He isn't taught anything new after a few

1. Esquire Magazine, May 1987, pp 114-116

weeks, he's just told to practice harder to perfect what he has already been shown. His enthusiasm drops rapidly. He gets bored. All of a sudden he begins to skip classes. The more classes one skips the easier they are to miss and the harder it is to pick up again. Then, when the Sensei calls to find out the problem, the inevitable rationalizations begin. "It's too hard", or "It's too easy", it's not what he had in mind…it's not practical, etc. He's decided to try something else that might better fulfill his desires, and special needs. If he's lucky, he might make it to a second plateau in this try, but then he'll probably give up and try something else.

It never ceases to amaze me at the number of students I encounter, who while interviewing concerning starting classes, have studied so many different martial arts. By the ripe old age of twenty-two or so, they've already studied Karate, Tae Kwon Do, some Kung Fu, a little Aikido, Judo, or Jujutsu, and are still looking for the perfect art. These people have reached the first plateau a dozen times or more and never seem to be able to continue in one discipline for any long period of time. They are "Dabblers" in the true sense of the word.

The second category referred to by Leonard as the "Obsessive" also applies to the student who takes up the martial arts. This is a "Type A" personality, i.e. goal oriented, hard-driving, perfectionist who "…knows that results are what counts." What is important is getting results fast, and in any way one can. This is the student who asks the instructor every question that pops into his head. He stays late after class, asks for references for books, videos, audio tapes, anything to get results quickly. The "Obsessive" student starts out with extremely noticeable progress until his plateau, usually about 2-3 months into training. He can't accept this leveling off position, and doubles his efforts. Introspection and patience are words foreign to his vocabulary. The instructor's admonitions and advice are ignored. Although he continues to make periodic short bursts of progress, they are always followed by a downward drop in function. When he finally becomes totally discouraged with his seeming "lack of progress" he usually quits, more times than not due to an injury.

I once had a student in one of my Karate classes who announced from the very beginning of training that one of his goals was to be able to break four or more boards with a punch in one strike. He had seen me do this at a demonstration, and it was one of the reasons he had come to see about taking Karate classes. I mentioned to him that by no means was that the purpose of studying Karate, and that my demonstration was only that, a demonstration showing the amount of power that might be generated through continual training. I told him in addition to developing the speed and power necessary to be able to break the boards, he had to develop focus and desensitize his knuckles with a gradual conditioning program. Further, I mentioned this is a long gradual process, with daily training required and many thousands of strikes on the makiwara (a forging board for the extremities). I also told him he should not be too over enthusiastic with this particular type of training because if not done properly he would actually slow his progress, and he could very well injure himself in the process. After about three months of Karate training, I said that if he still wished to train for Tameshiwari (Breaking), that he could began. He was elated! I reiterated to him the program of conditioning I wished him to follow and reminded him if he did not follow this program he would injure himself. After two weeks of striking the Makiwara, doing pushups on his knuckles, using special liniment to condition and rejuvenate the skin, he felt he was ready for bigger fish. He had been striking the post with a canvas pad attached, and said he did not feel any pain and was ready to break. I disagreed with him, but he was ready for a different striking surface. I then moved the straw striking pad into place to allow him to begin working on this pad with 20 strikes each day, full power, and adding five per day until he reached 200 strikes. At this time he would be ready to try a multiple board break. Well, as one might have guessed, he went from 20 strikes on the first day to 100 strikes on the third day. The skin on his knuckles was torn to the bone. He was in such pain, he could barely make a fist, let alone strike any surface harder than cotton. I told him it would be at least a month before I would let him resume his training and then he would have to begin on the canvas pad again. After 10 days when the knuckles had gotten a good scab on them, he decided he was ready. He approached the makiwara, struck it with one powerful blow and shattered the middle knuckle of his right forefist. I picked him up, iced his hand and told him he had just ended his own training. He stayed for the rest of class but never came back. His tunnel vision and obsession was his own downfall.

The third type of individual in the Leonard article is the "Hacker". This student will learn a few basic principles, or techniques, and be satisfied with his progress. He remains on the plateau for an extended period of time. The things he does wrong prevent him from ever becoming more than average. He still makes the same mistakes he made four months earlier but they are now virtually impossible to correct and thus he can't understand why he doesn't advance his rank. The extra time spent training is always on something new or different rather than on the trouble areas of his own training. The "Hacker" is definitely not on the road to mastery and will eventually quit because of boredom or frustration; he figures he's learned all that he can, anything else is of little consequence. These individuals are sometimes the same who will start his own "style" based on the way he performs a certain technique or principle rather than the way it is supposed to be done.

The road to mastery of the martial arts must be one of striving to hone the basic skills, not with the goal of "mastery" in mind. Rather the training itself is the self-satisfying experience. The temporary plateau is looked upon as an opportunity to polish skills already learned, in anticipation of greater insight and being "ready" to learn new skills. The most difficult part of the road to mastery is just simply staying on the road. All other setbacks aside, he who has no self-centered goal of accomplishment, is the one who really becomes the master. In the words of the 19th century Samurai-TessHu:

> *"Do not think that this is all there is.*
> *More and more wonderful teachings exist*
> *The sword is unfathomable."*

In the art of Kenjutsu (fighting with the sword), the student bases all his actions on the sword; every movement is related to the action of the sword. Every waking moment he has the sword in mind, until after many years, there is no difference between the student and the sword…the student is the sword! He is straight, cold, tempered from training, able to defeat any situation, and defeated by none. His actions are totally impersonal. Just as the sword cuts without thought as to who or what it is cutting, the Kenjutsuka merely responds to the situation at hand, and does what has to be done to bring forth a restoration of balance. Hardships, threatening situations, dangers, or setbacks are nothing more than the natural balance of things slightly out of kilter. This is a very simple matter of concerning oneself with restoring the "balance". This is as true in physical confrontations as it is in the treatment of illnesses based on the oriental theory of medicine applied in both Acupuncture and Acupressure (Shiatsu). When the body's natural energy balance (Yin/Yang or In/Yo in Japanese) is out of kilter or disturbed, it shows up as either as excess in one area or a deficiency in another. Theoretically, equalizing this imbalance is what restores health to the body. In training for martial arts, the same theory of

In/Yo applies. Excessive training in one facet of training (necessarily causing a lack of training in another area) results in an individual who is good at one thing but lousy at another rather than a well rounded, evenly trained individual capable of performing a variety of techniques. This has happened in modern Judo to a great degree. Emphasis on form and a well rounded variety of techniques has given way to the idea of working on only a few favorite techniques for tournament use, the goal being to score a point.

The well-rounded Judoka is hard to find these days. Today's Judoka generally has developed two to four techniques that he can do well, and has ignored all the others. Just as a body builder must work all portions of his body equally, a poor body builder may have 21 inch arms, coupled with 18 inch thighs and is labeled as "chicken legs" by his workout partners. The weak areas sometimes require twice as much work just to be brought up to the level of the average areas. The big winners in the body building contests are not necessarily the biggest in bulk or even definition; more often than not "proportional development" is what makes the winner. Equal dedication and work to all parts of the body…symmetry!

To become a master of Hakkoryu Jujutsu, work all the techniques! Do not work only on your favorite techniques or the ones which don't hurt as much. Work the hardest techniques twice as often as the easy ones; start with them and finish with them. Increase your pain tolerance a little bit more with each practice session. Don't just tap out as soon as a technique is put on. See what you can really take (without injuring yourself of course). These are all way stations on the road to mastery. Unfortunately there are few shortcuts. We must all pay the toll on the turnpike, if you don't, you just can't get through Pennsylvania!

❂ *Chapter Three* ❂

Walking Exercises

As a general rule, the walking exercises as presented in this book and the previous two books on Hakkoryu Jujutsu, are not considered a "standard" part of the system as taught at the headquarters (Hombu) in Japan. They are, however, a series of exercises developed over a period of fifteen years designed to allow the student to acquire and develop basic abilities of movement; tai sabaki; practice in rolling; avoidance; and body positioning.

Just the ability to "walk" properly in a "martial way" is something most people will never have the opportunity to develop. These exercises, therefore, attempt to fill that void in training from the mastery of the "kihon" basics, to the eventual application of these waza if necessary. At the higher level of these exercises (i.e. 5B - 8B, and 5C - 8C) as illustrated in this book, the student is introduced to a series of basic movements that are also designed to instill principles of response for attacks from the rear, frontal kicks, and up close-surprise assaults. These applications are fully illustrated in this chapter in basic form, and in "bunkai", the application.

Walking Exercises 5B - 8B

Exercise 5B. A defense against a knife or arm attack from the rear. In this exercise, Tori turns, keeping his arm low (depending upon where the weapon is held against his back) as he slides away slightly, pushing the arm holding the weapon aside. He then bends his arm at the elbow, securing the hand holding the weapon to his upper arm. He then steps through with a Tegatana (sword hand) strike to the shoulder, and drops the attacker to the rear, retaining control of the weapon. The weapon can be removed after the takedown. (Photos 1-4 and 5-7 Bunkai)

Walking Exercise 5B (continued)

1

2

3

4

Bunkai

5

6

7

Exercise 6B. A defense against a rear weapon attack from the outside.
Here the Tori again turns with his arm swinging low, deflecting the weapon holding arm; he then slides in close, placing his arm around the neck and under the arm of the attacker. Stepping in further with his rear leg, he secures the attacker's neck and applies a choke with the inside of his forearm against the carotid artery. Stepping back around, he turns and drops to one knee taking down the assailant, and choking him into submission if necessary. (Photos 1 - 5 and 6 - 9 Bunkai)

1

2

3

4   5

Bunkai

6

7

8

9

Exercise 7B. A defense aaainst a front kick to the groin. Using an "X" block, "Juji Uke", Tori blocks the oncoming kick. He then opens his hands and, with one hand at the ankle and the other at the knee, he turns the attacker around by rotating the hands to the outside. He then pulls in toward his waist, causing the attacker to drop to the ground, After the fall, he can finish up with a strike to the groin if desired. (Photos 1 - 5 and 6 - 10 Bunkai)

1

2

3

4

5

Bunkai

6

7

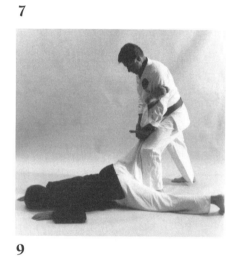

8

9

10

Exercise 8B. A defense against a close grab and pull. Here, Tori is grabbed from the side. He moves with the pull; pulling his grabbed hand in slightly, using the little finger side of the hand and executes an elbow strike to the face followed by another to the side of the head. This is a quick and effective escape and counter technique. (Photos 1 - 4 and 5 - 8 Bunkai)

1

2

3

4

Bunkai

5

6

7

8

Walking Exercises 5C - 8C

Exercise 5C. A defense from the rear two handed grabbing attack. Tori is approached from the rear by a person attempting to grab him with both hands. He turns, raising both hands above his head and strikes downward with Tegatana strike against the inside of the wrists of Kake. He then strikes the groin and face simultaneously using the palm heels of both hands; grabs the pants and steps forward, pulling the low hand and pushing the upper hand, dropping the Kake to the rear, he follows up immediately with a Tegatana strike to the groin. (Photos 1 - 5 and 6 - 10 Bunkai)

1

2

3

4

5

Bunkai

6

7

8

9

10

Exercise 6C. A defense against a rear weapon attack from the outside.
Tori pivots to the outside on his rear foot, dropping his arm to deflect the
weapon away. He simultaneously delivers a middle knuckle strike (Naka Yubi
Ken) to the ribs of the Kake. He then grabs the attacker's arm and stepping
through with his rear leg, he throws the Kake forward using Mae Otoshi (front
drop) and secures the weapon at the same time. (Photos 1 - 4 and 5 - 8 Bunkai)

1

2

3

4

Bunkai

5

6

7

8

Exercise 7C. A defense against an up close kick to the groin. Tori blocks the coming kick by shifting his weight to his back leg, and raising his front leg to protect his groin area, while simultaneously executing Metsubushi to the attacker's face. He then steps back with his lead foot and performs a Senpenbanka strike to the face. Stepping through, he executes Naka Yubi Ken on the sternum of the attacker, pushing him away to the rear. (Photos 1 - 5 and 6 - 9 Bunkai)

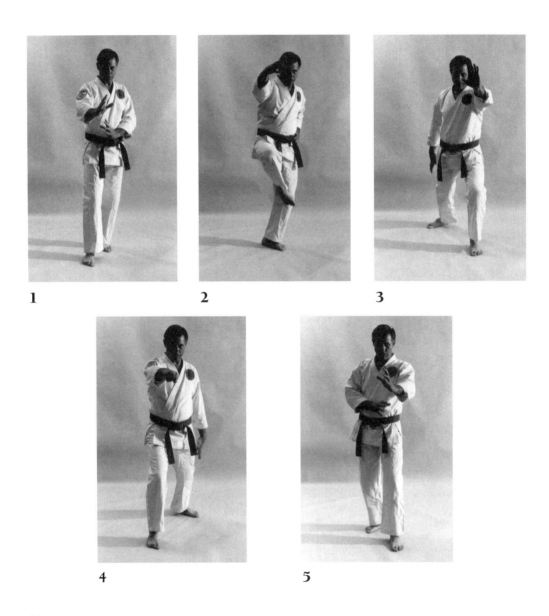

1   2   3

4   5

Bunkai

6

7

8

9

Exercise 8C. The last in this series is a defense against an up close two handed grab by the Kake. Tori deflects the grab with both hands turned outward with the palms up. He then grips Kake's wrists, pulling them down as he executes first a knee strike to the solar plexus, followed immediately by an instep strike to the groin (Kin Geri). He then pushes Kake away and resumes a ready stance. (Photos 1 - 7 and 8 - 11 Bunkai)

These last eight walking exercises can be very useful and practical when practiced regularly. The attacks are relatively common and allow minimal response to a threatening situation. These are usually practiced as a group at the beginning of class.

1   2   3   4

5   6   7

Bunkai

8

9

10

11

❖ *Chapter Four* ❖

Special Training Exercises

Although HAKKORYU Jujutsu is generally looked upon as a "responsive" type of martial art, i.e., waiting until the aggressor makes the first move, by no means is that the proper attitude in the realm of personal self-protection. As in Karate, the saying "Karate ni sente nashi" (In Karate there is no first attack), should not be misconstrued as meaning one must wait for the other person to attack, physically, before defending oneself. Once the intent is made by an aggressor, the "attack" for all practical purposes has been made. Of course, the ability to discern this intent is not easily acquired. It takes many years of practice and specialized training to develop this ability. In Hakkoryu the same principle is true. One need not wait until physically attacked before responding. The sixth sense is the level of insight that can only be imagined by most students of the martial arts, but one which we should all strive for.

In a situation where either because of the attitude of the other person, or just the sheer number of aggressors, it is blatantly obvious that you are in danger of being attacked; it is at this moment that you must act. You have sensed that the aggressor is ready to make his move (the threat of the intent) and you react accordingly and hopefully, appropriately. It might be something as simple as opening a door, walking through it and closing it behind you. It might also be as subtle as taking your gaze away from the attacker's eyes and momentarily looking away, or over his shoulder, distracting him and allowing you to escape. Escape is nothing to be ashamed of…not knowing what to do at the time is!

The various methods of striking in self defense involve use of the Tegatana (sword hand strike), Naka Yubi Ken (middle knuckle strike), Teisho (palm heel strike), Kakuto (chicken head strike), Hiji Ate (elbow strike), Hiza Ate (knee strike), Mae Geri (front snap kick), Fumi Komi (stomping kick), Atama Ate (head strike), Tettsui Uchi (hammer fist), and Ashi Ate (inside foot strike).

Many of these striking applications are reserved for situations against multiple attackers although the intent of Soke Okuyama, in the formulation of Hakkoryu, was that his students and practitioners be able to defend themselves regardless of the situation. The mastery of basic waza was intended to give proficiency and a command of basic principles, the final application of which remains with the student and his own moral ethics. To misuse or overuse these techniques merely for the purpose of inflicting pain or punishment was never the intention of Master Okuyama. We all recognize there are times, however, that an individual when faced with overwhelming odds is totally justified in using extraordinary means to defend himself, his loved ones and friends; it is then, and only then, that many of these additional methods of striking are justifiably brought into play. Some of them can be quite devastating if properly applied, and others, a complete surprise to the attacker. I urge you now - exercise caution while training in these methods of "defensive attack" lest you injure your training partner.

These particular striking methods should be studied and practiced in conjunction with learning the various vital areas (kyusho) to strike for the greatest effect. For example (Photo H) using the Tegatana to strike the Hai Kei (Lung Line Kyusho) can cause extreme pain, making the person's hand open, and momentarily numbing or paralyzing the arm or hand. Using the Oya Yubi (thumb), or Naka Yubi strike (Photo I) to the centerline point on the conception meridian can also have paralyzing effects, and spontaneous release of a grip or hold. Strikes to the Dai Cho Kei (Large Intestine Kyusho) can be extremely painful, bringing a person to their knees, as is illustrated in the use of the GAKUN grip used extensively in Sandan Gi waza. Accuracy and the proper strike are more important than the power of the strike. Some areas should be struck quickly while others merely pushed or pressed for effect. Examples of these striking methods and applications are illustrated in photos J through L.

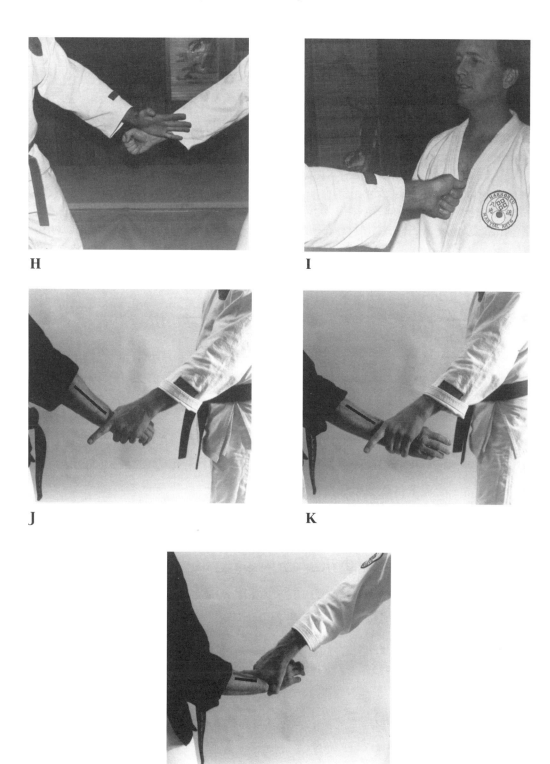

H

I

J

K

L

Happo No Sabaki
Eight directional movement exercise

This extremely useful movement exercise is simple and can be one of the most important exercises to learn. It allows the student to move, guard, defend, attack, and parry in all eight directions of possible attack. Once the direction of movement is learned, it can easily be applied to practice with such weapons as the Bo, Jo, Hanbo, Nunchaku, or virtually any weapon with which a person is trying to become proficient. When done properly to either the right or left side (based on which foot begins the exercise), the pivot, or back, foot should remain in the same position for the entire exercise. The following illustration shows the movements numbered in the proper sequence for starting the exercise by stepping out with the left foot, from an attention or Musubi Dachi stance. You may step in T-Dachi, Zenkutsu Dachi (forward leaning stance), Kokutsu Dachi (back stance), or any stance you wish.

Using the points of the compass as a reference:

1. Step with the left foot;

2. Pivot 180° to face position 2;

3. Move the left foot out 90° to face position 3;

4. Move the left foot back 45° to allow you to face position 4;

5. Step through with the left foot, turning to the right and face position 5;

6. Step out 45° to face position 6;

7. Turn right 180° to face position 7;

8. Turn left with the left foot 90° to face position 8; and finally,

9. End by withdrawing the left foot, to the starting position.

Repeat the exercise starting with the right foot and change number 3 to 8 to coincide with doing the exercise on the opposite side. I think you will find that this valuable exercise has many applications in your training.

Happo No Sabaki
Eight directional movement exercise

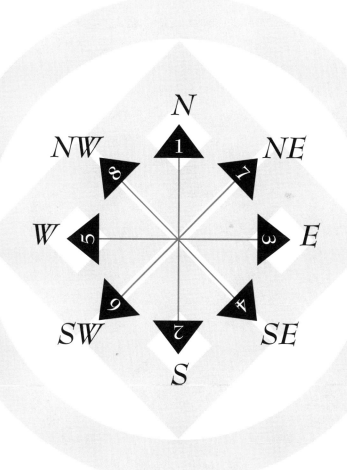

❖ *Chapter Five* ❖

Techniques of Sandan Gi

MAJOR PRINCIPLES

1. Mochi Maware   2. Gakun   3. Maki Komi   4. Te Kagami

	Principle	Meaning
Suware Waza		
1. Ude OsaeDori	Mochi Maware	Shoulder Pin Art
2. Muni Osae Dori	Mochi Maware	Chest/Lapel Pin Art
3. Uchi Komi Dori	Gakun	Overhand Strike Art
4. Te Kagami	The Grip	Hand Mirror
5. Kata Mune Osae Aya Dori	Gakun	Woven Cloth Art
Hantachi Waza		
6. Yoko Dori	Maki Komi	Side Attack Art
7. Morote Osae Dori	Te Kagami	Two Hand Pin Art
8. Ushiro Gyaku Kube Shime Dori	Gakun/Mochi Maware	Rear Reverse Neck Choke
Tachi Waza		
9. Rio Mune Osae Dori	Mochi Maware	Two Hand Chest/Lapel Art
10. Emon Dori	Mochi Maware	Top of Shoulder Grab
11. Tachi Te Kagami	Te Kagami	Hand Mirror
12. Uchi Komi Dori	Gakun	Overhand Strike Art
13. Tsuki Mi Dori	Gakun	Body Thrust Art
14. Kata Mune Osae Mochi Maware	Gakun/Mochi Maware	Chest Grab
15. Riote Mochi Maware	Mochi Maware Gatame	Two Handed Lead Around
16. Ushiro Zeme Dori	Mochi Maware	Rear Attack Art
17. Ushiro Emon Dori	Gakun/Mochi Maware	Rear Shoulder Grab
18. Ushiro Obi Hiki Dori	Mochi Maware	Rear Belt Grab
19. Mae Obi Hiki Dori	Mochi Maware	Front Belt Grab
20. Nuki Uchi Dori	Gakun	Sword Draw/Strike Art
21. Tsukko Mi Dori	Gakun	Knife Thrust Art
22. Ushiro Hakko Dori	Mochi Maware	Rear Eighth Light Art

THE WAZA OF SANDAN GI

Suware Waza:

1. Ude Osae Dori: Kake grabs Tori by the sleeve (Photo 1). Tori pins the hand and applies the basic armbar as in Nidan (Photo 2). After forcing Kake to release and bend down, Tori changes his gripping hands and turns Kake around using the Mochi Maware principle. He then finishes the technique with a lock below the shoulder blade of Kake. (Photo 4 and close-up)

1

2

3

4

Close-up

2. Mune Osae Dori: Grabbed on the chest or lapel, Tori again secures the hand so that Kake can't release his grip. He performs the Nidan wrist bend and, after forcing Kake down and releasing his grip, he changes hand grips again turning Kake around using the Mochi Maware principle, and locks the arm behind the back. (Photos 1-4)

1

2

3

4

3. Uchi Komi Dori: As Kake strikes downward with force, Tori deflects this downward force and this time applies the GAKUN grip to the inside radial bone of Kake. Applying pressure downward, Tori then pulls Kake forward, pinning him to the mat with the downward pressure of GAKUN, using his body to apply the pressure while simultaneously delivering an Atemi strike to the ribs. (Photos 1-3 and close-up)

1

2

3

Close up

4. Te Kagami: Grabbed by both wrists, Tori applies Te Kagami as in Nidan waza. However, instead of causing Kake to fall to the side, Tori takes Kake straight down between his legs and applies the locking pin to Kake's wrist while using his forearm across the back of his neck to hold him in place. (Photos 1-4 and close up)

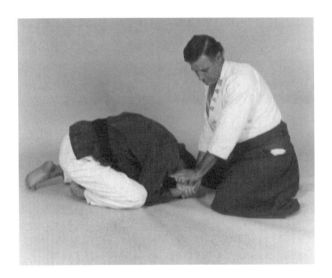

1

2

3

4

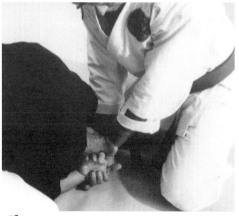

Close-up

5. Kata Mune Osae Aya Dori: Kake grabs Tori by the lapel. Tori grabs the first two fingers of Kake's free hand and pulls the fingers and hand across the front of Kake's body bending the fingers backwards. Once the hand is across, Tori then applies GAKUN to the radial bone of Kake's left wrist, forcing him down, then finishes with a GAKUN pin and Atemi strike to the ribs. (Photos 1-4 and close ups)

1

2

2 - Close up

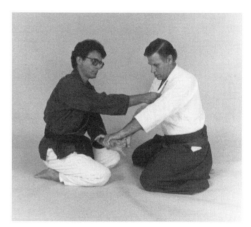

3

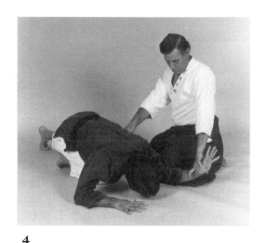

4

4 - Close-up

6. Yoko Katate Dori: Kake grabs Tori's hand from the side in an attempt to strike him. Tori thwarts this attempt by raising his hand, nullifying the pull and blocking the strike. While holding Kake's hand firmly with the left hand, he then rotates his right hand backwards and around the front. Tori brings Kake down to his face, pinning him with his knee in the shoulder joint, while bending his wrist inward toward Kake's head. Pressure should be applied simultaneously to the three areas, i.e., shoulder joint, wrist, and back of wrist with sword hand. NOTE: THIS IS A VERY PAINFUL, FINISHING PIN. (Photos 1-4 and close-up)

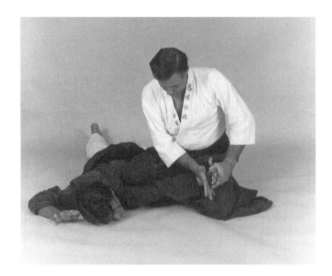

1

2

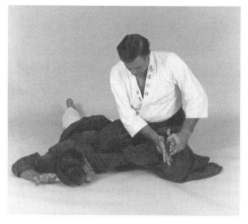

3

2 - close up

7. Morote Osae Dori: Grabbed from the side by two hands and pulled, Tori stops the pull by raising his hand and lowering his elbow. He then takes a grip on the left hand of Kake, and applies the Te Kagami grip and principle. He pulls Kake down in front of him and, placing his elbow between his knees, continues to apply the Te Kagami pin. NOTE: THIS IS ALSO A VERY PAINFUL FINISHING PIN. (Photos 1-4 and close-up)

1

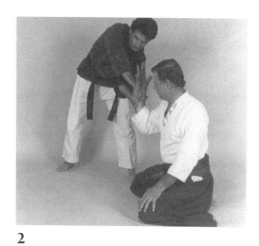

2

3

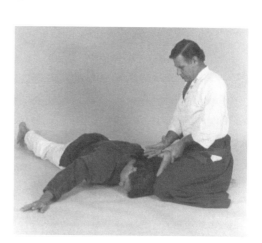

4

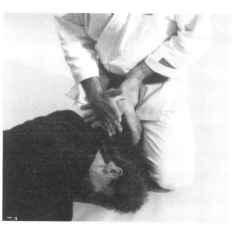

4 - close up

8. Ushiro Gyaku Kube Shime Dori: Escape from a rear armbar and choke. Kake attacks Tori from behind, barring his arm, and choking him by grabbing his lapel and pulling back across his neck. Tori brings his chin down, and drops his right arm, breaking the armbar hold. He then brings Kake's right hand around to the front and applies GAKUN to the outside edge (Ulnar) of Kake's wrist. Applying steady Gakun pressure to the wrist and using his own right arm to lever Kake back, around and behind him, Tori then switches to a painful wrist bend for the start of the Mochi Maware take around (see close-ups). Bringing Kake around to the front, he applies the finishing SANDAN lock behind the back. (Photos 1-6 and close-ups)

1

2

2 - close up

3

4

5

5 - close up

6

Tachi Waza

9. Rio Mune Osae Dori: Kake attacks by grabbing both lapels of Tori. Tori reaches over the top of both arms and applies the Nidan wrist lock on Kake, forcing him to release his grip and causing him to move back and away in pain. He then switches hands and applies the lock to Kake's wrist, pushing his hand into Kake's face, unbalancing him to the rear. Turning his wrist downward and to the front, Kake is placed into a circular spin around to the front by Tori, and then locked out in the SANDAN lock of Mochi Maware. (Photos 1-7 and close-ups)

1

2

3

4

5

6

6 - close up

7

7 - close up

10. Emon Dori: Front shoulder or epaulet grab. Kake grabs Tori on the top of the shoulder and attempts to strike him. Tori applies Metsubushi (Photo 1), then pins the hand to his shoulder. Keeping the hand tightly pinned to the top of the shoulder, Tori bends forward as if to touch his left shoulder to Kake's left knee thereby causing extreme pain to the attacker. He then changes hand grips and executes the Mochi Maware finish by bringing Kake down, around, and back up to finish with the SANDAN lock. (Photos 1-7)

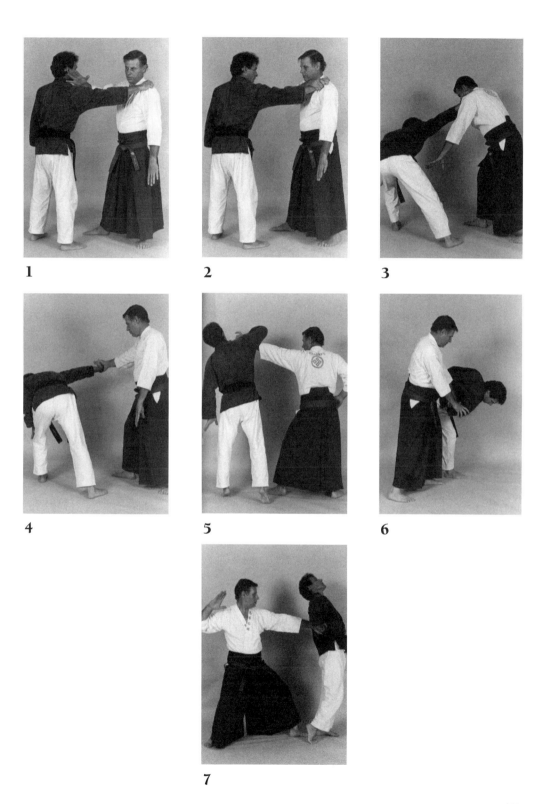

1

2

3

4

5

6

7

11. Tachi Te Kagami: Grabbed by both hands, Tori applies Te Kagami release. Instead of throwing Kake to the side, as in Shodan and Nidan versions, he uses both hands to bring Kake straight down to the ground, pivoting clockwise on his left foot. He then pins Kake's hand to the ground with his left foot and stands to complete the technique. (Photos 1-4 and close-up of pin)

1

2

3

4

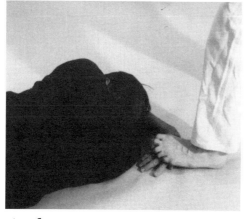

4 - close up

12. Uchi Komi Dori: Just as in waza #3 earlier, Kake strikes downward to hit Tori. Tori intercepts and deflects the strike but applies GAKUN to the inside (radial) of Kake's wrist. He pushes down and outward with the GAKUN and steps back with his left leg, going to his knee and finishes with the GAKUN pin using his body weight to apply additional pressure to the grip. (Photos 1-3 and close up)

1

2

3

3 - close up

13. Tsuki Mi Dori: Thrust to the body defense. As Kake steps in to attack Tori with a thrust strike to the body, Tori either catches the strike (Photo 2) or deflects the strike with Tegatana (Photo 3). He then applies GAKUN to the inside (radial) of Kake's wrist pushing inward and, continuing to apply the GAKUN, forces Kake down on his face in extreme pain. Tori then finishes with the GAKUN pin as he steps back with his lead leg. (Photos 1-5 and close-ups)

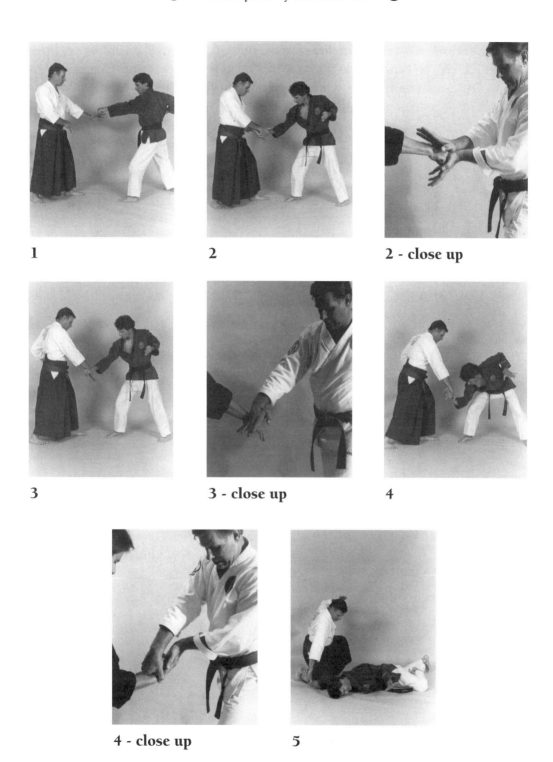

1

2

2 - close up

3

3 - close up

4

4 - close up

5

14. Kata Mune Osae Mochi Maware: Grabbed on the chest by Kake, Tori secures Kake's free hand and applies GAKUN. He then lifts the arm, steps under and applies Atemi to the ribs with his elbow and finishes with Mochi Maware. (Photos 1-6)

1

2

3

4

5

6

15. Riote Mochi Maware: Two handed lead around and pin. Anticipating an attack by Kake, Tori takes the initiative by grabbing both of Kake's wrists after executing a double Metsubushi strike to distract. He grabs and applies GAKUN to both wrists. Continuing the pressure downward with one hand and pushing the other hand into Kake's face, he causes Kake to fall to the ground on his side. (Photo 7) Then, placing one hand under the upper arm of the other with the little finger side of the hand pushing into the back of the triceps muscle of the other arm, (see close-up), Tori pushes down with the arm applying GAKUN to the inside (radial) portion of Kake's wrist simultaneously placing his knee against the trapped hand and effecting an armbar. This is a very, very painful pin and lockout. Kake can tap for release only with his feet. (Photos 1-7 and close-up)

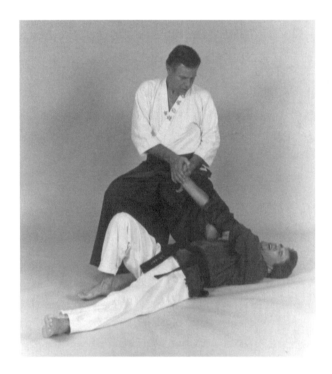

1

2

3

4

5

6

7

7 - close up

16. Ushiro Zeme Dori: Rear attack. Grabbed from behind around the upper body and arms, Tori expands his presence by lifting his chest upward, moving his arms outward and leaning slightly backwards. He then drops his weight quickly and stepping out to the side of Kake's top hand, he executes GAKUN against the outside (ulnar) portion of Kake's left wrist, while using his own left arm to form an armbar against the GAKUN grip. This forces Kake around behind Tori and allows Tori to execute the Mochi Maware spin around and lock. (Photos 1-6)

1

2

3

4

5

6

17. Ushiro Emon Dori: Rear shoulder grab. Grabbed on the top of the left shoulder, Tori secures Kake's hand as he steps slightly away pulling Kake off balance. As he turns back in, to face Kake, he drops his weight low and applies a very painful GAKUN to the outside (ulnar) of Kake's left wrist. He then steps under the arm executing an elbow Atemi to his ribs and continues the waza with the Mochi Maware take around and lock. (Photos 1-7)

1

2

3

4

5

6

7

18. Ushiro Obi Hiki Dori: Defense against a rear belt grab or pickpocket. Grabbing Tori's belt from the rear, Kake attempts to pull him or steal his wallet. Tori turns and quickly executes Metsubushi to Kake's face, and immediately secures Kake's hand in position. He then applies the GAKUN grip to the outside (ulnar) of Kake's wrist and using his body weight again, forces Kake to release his grip. The waza continues with Tori again moving under the arm, applying Atemi, and finishing the SANDAN lock. (Photos 1-5)

1

2

3

4   5

l9. Mae Obi Hiki Dori: Front belt grab and pull. Grabbing Kake's belt from the front and pulling, Tori secures both wrists and applies GAKUN. Each GAKUN is accompanied by a step on the same side adding to the pressure and the resultant pain of the grip. After unbalancing Kake with the GAKUN and causing him to release his grips, Tori continues the technique by releasing one of his grips, moving under Kake's secured arm and again finishing with the Mochi Maware ending as in earlier waza. (Photos 1-7)

1

2

3

4

5

5

7

20. Nuki Uchi Dori: Defense against a sword draw. Kake draws his sword in attempt to cut down Tori with a single cut. Tori moves in toward the right shoulder of Kake, by pivoting on his left foot, 90° clockwise, while at the same time using his left hand to stop the cutting action of the sword. (Photo 2) He then applies GAKUN to the inside of Kake's wrist from the top, pushing inward and down. Continuing this GAKUN pressure, Tori pivots to his right forcing Kake down, and immobilizing the sword. He then places his knee in the shoulder joint securing the arm. He then removes the sword and applies TSUKA ATE to Kake's head. (Photos 1- 5)

1

2

3

4

5

21. Tsukkomi Mi Dori: Defense against knife thrust/slash. Kake draws his blade and attempts to cut Tori. As in Nuki Uchi, Tori stops the slash with his left hand and moves to the outside. Applying GAKUN again he forces Kake down with his turn and finishes with the pin similar to Nuki Uchi. (Photos 1-4 and close up)

1

2

3

3 - close up

4

5

22. Ushiro Hakko Dori: Kake attacks Tori by grabbing both his arms from behind in an attempt to stop him or pull him. Tori steps back into Kake, bending forward, dropping his weight and forcing his hands upward toward Kake's face. Kake is unable to hold on at this point which allows Tori to break free and apply GAKUN to the wrist and to follow up the technique with the Mochi Maware and SANDAN lock used extensively in Sandan Gi. (Photos 1-5)

1

2

3

4

5

23. Tachi Matsuba Dori: Standing pine needle break. Grabbed by both wrists, Tori applies Matsuba Dori (as in Nidan waza). After the release, he changes his grip and again continues the waza with the Mochi Maware follow up and lock out. (Photos 1- 5)

1

2

3

4

5

24. Variation on Tsuki Mi Dori (Waza 13): Instead of attempting to catch a punch thrown at the head, Tori merely deflects the punch with Tegatana, applies GAKUN to the inside of the wrist, pushes downward and continues the GAKUN forcing Kake to his face while stepping back. (Photos 1-3)

1

2

3

25. Variation on Tsukkomi Dori: Knife slash art. After stopping the attack and applying GAKUN (Photo 3), Tori steps behind Kake making an armbar against his own upper body using his left hand under Kake's chin. He pulls his hands in opposite directions putting extreme pressure on the elbow, shoulder, and neck of Kake, causing him to submit and drop the weapon. (Photos 1-4)

1

2

3

4

Second variation on knife slash art: After stopping the initial cutting action and applying GAKUN to Kake's wrist, Tori then bends Kake's wrist inward, bringing the cutting edge of the blade to rest against Kake's throat while securing Kake's left arm with his left arm and causing Kake to submit or be cut. (Photos 1-3)

1

2

3

Third variation on knife slash art: After again stopping the cutting action of Kake, Tori bends Kake's wrist inward as he steps to the front of Kake. Using his body weight, he drops to his knee with Kake's arm and knife secured forcing Kake down on his back. Tori causes Kake to drop the knife by bending his wrist against the floor and, taking control of the knife, finishes the technique. (Photo 1-4)

1

2

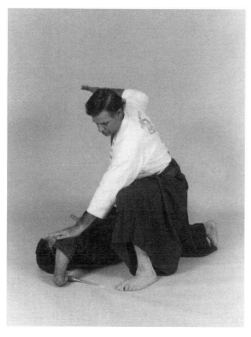

3

4

Notes to this Section

1. In Hakkoryu this ability of "Thought Transference" or comprehension of intentions without speaking, is known as ISHIN DENSHIN. This is considered to be one of the ultimate accomplishments of the Hakkoryu Shihan, and is an area he must strive to develop, much on his own, with the guidance of the Soke. However, even with his guidance, much continual practice, and training is required to develop this trait.

2. GAKUN is the Hakkoryu Grip. Translated, literally it means "special" or "effective" grip. Although this grip is called by the same name in Nidan and Shodan waza, it is quite different in the Sandan application. At this level, it does not necessarily involve the bending of the wrist as in Shodan and Nidan, rather it is a grip on the top of the hand and wrist, using the base of the index finger to apply Atemi waza to the vital points on the inside and outside of the wrist (Large and Small Intestine meridians). When applied properly the pain is very great with immediate results to the aggressor.

❀ *Chapter Six* ❀

Amma and Igaku Massage

This section will deal with IGAKU SHIATSU, a subject which was very dear to the founder of HAKKORYU. Since it would be impractical to attempt to teach Shiatsu (acupressure) in one small section of this book, the illustrations and explanations will be rather brief. These are given primarily to allow the student to perform a simple type of acupressure massage (AMMA) on his fellow students or relatives after a good workout or to relieve daily tensions and fatigue in the body. The massage techniques illustrated in this section fall into the category of "AMMA" or pressure rubbing massage which is used to sooth irritated nerves and revitalize sluggish bodily functions. This is done by pressing, squeezing, and rubbing primarily the muscular areas around Tsubos, and manipulating the body joints. This technique along with a sprinkling of Koho Igaku Shiatsu will allow the student to provide a pleasant, therapeutic massage to his or her partner with beneficial results. This massage is best done after workouts when the body is warm, loosened up, and generally much more relaxed than at the beginning of training. It can be performed at any time but should be at least 1 to 1 1/2 hours after eating a full meal. It is also excellent after taking a warm bath and relaxing the body. The techniques of applying pressure will involve the use of the thumb, palm heel, edge of the hand, fingers, and the knuckles of the hand.

Procedure

Shiatsu can be performed in various orders of arrangement. However, I will ask you to perform the treatment in the following manner, under the supposition that you will be doing a "full body" treatment, vis-a-vis just working on an injured or strained area of the body. The order is: (1) back, (2) back of legs, (3) front of legs, (4) feet, (5) abdomen, (6) chest, (7) neck and shoulders. A full Shiatsu treatment by a certified practitioner takes from

45 minutes to an hour or more.

(1) The Back

Have the recipient lie on his stomach with the head turned comfortably to either side (Photos 1 & 2). Kneel at the head and begin by slowly and gently rubbing and massaging the back muscles to loosen them up, working from the larger muscles between the shoulders, outward and downward to the smaller muscles of the waist. You will now begin using the thumbs to apply pressure. NOTE: The pressure should be applied with the pad of the thumb, not the tip. Also, keep the arms straight and use the entire body to apply the pressure, not just the fingers. Always direct the pressure toward the center of the body.

(Photo 3) Beginning at approximately the center of the shoulder blades, with both thumbs, on either side of the spine (NEVER DIRECTLY ON THE SPINE), move downward along the muscles, approximately one thumb width each time, until reaching the lowest portion of the lumbar area (waist). Upon reaching the lower portion, cup the left hand and tapping with the heel of the right, move upward along the spine. Repeat the procedure three times.

(Photo 4) Next, using the thumbs, press gently around the outline of the shoulder blade, three times, from the inside toward the armpit and then from the inside edge of the shoulder blade, using 1 thumb, begin pressing and applying pressure the full length of the trunk to the waist three times. Do this again on the opposite side. After completing this procedure, place both hands on the sides of the body and vigorously rub up and down for a few second.

(Photo 5) For the lower back, using the thumbs, start on either side of the lower spine and move both hands outward together, again about one thumb width and repeat again. Perform each line three times.

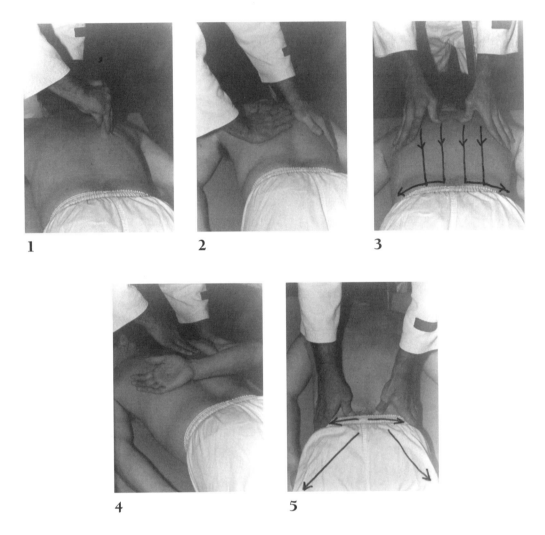

1

2

3

4

5

(2) Back Of Legs

This area of the legs is one that is often quite sensitive to thumb pressure because the muscles tend to contract, especially in individuals who do a lot of running or jogging. For this reason, a modifled method of massage is shown here. First, have the individual relax the leg and, holding the ankle, bend the leg at the knee. This helps to relax the large biceps muscle of the thigh and minimizes the pain from the pressure. Instead of using the thumb, begin by using the knuckles of the fist as illustrated (Photo 6), and gently knead the muscles from the base of the buttocks downward to the knee, stopping at the knee. Repeat this three times. At the knee, using one thumb, GENTLY massage the back of the knee with only a very light pressure. Moving to the calf, begin by massaging the muscles between the thumb and the four fingers and gently squeezing and lifting the muscles. Follow this with the thumb application three times to the ankle. Then using the knuckles of the hand, apply weight directly to the bottom of the foot (Plantar arch), slightly pressing in with the knuckles and massage with a vibrating motion. This section should be repeated on the opposite leg. (Photos 7 & 8)

6

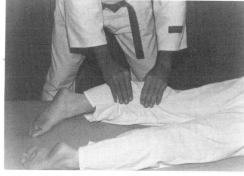

7

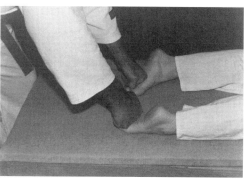

8

(3) Front of Legs

The legs contain three very important meridians for Shiatsu work; the Gall Bladder Meridian which is down the side of the leg; the Liver Meridian located up the inside of the shin and thigh and; the Kidney Meridian which is also up the inside of the leg, shin, and thigh. Parallel to these is the Spleen Meridian (Photo 9). Pressure of the thumbs on these meridians can be quite painful if not exerted properly. Therefore, only a squeezing type of massage should be used by the student for this "Amma" technique. Beginning at the top of the thigh, massage by squeezing the thumb and four fingers together from the ankle to the top of the thigh along the larger muscle groups. This will help to relax stiff and tired muscles of the leg. Continue by doing a circular massaged on the front of the thigh muscles two to three times.

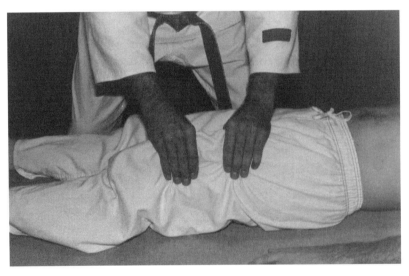

9

(4) Stomach/Adominal Area

When working on this area, it is recommended you have the person lift their knees and bend their legs so as to relax the abdominal muscles more easily and allow for a more comfortable massage of the abdomen.

(Photo 10) Begin by using three fingers, the index, middle, and ring, to move around the outer edge of the pelvis. Apply pressure gently in these areas. There should be no sharp or severe pain experienced. If there is, examination by a doctor might be warranted. When you get to the lower area of the abdomen, switch from the finger tips to the palm heel of the hand, which must be above the pubic bone and apply pressure slowly but rather firmly. Continue up the right side of the abdominal cavity, using the three fingers again, under the rib cage, returning to the center starting point. (Photo 11) After the first cycle around the cavity, using the thumb and fingers, gently knead the stomach area from the outside inward, squeezing and lifting 2 to 3 times on each side. Repeat the same cycle again, this time using two fingers and the third time using only the thumb for pressure, except at the lower portion where the palm heel should be used each time.

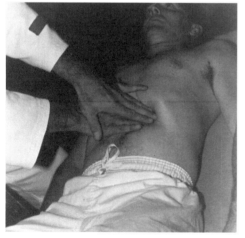

10

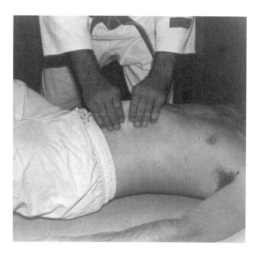

11

(5) The Feet

Moving downward to the feet (Photo 12) gently knead the feet with the thumb and fingers flexing the ankle joint upward and downward (extended position) several times to relax the ankle and foot muscles. If desired you may wish to "crack" the toes; starting with the smallest, holding it gently between the thumb and index finger, wiggling it easily, and then pulling gently. If the toe does not "crack" easily do not force it. It is sometimes difficult to crack the large toe, so do not force it.

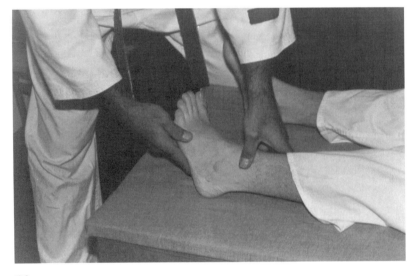

12

(6) Chest

Have the person roll over and lie on his back with the arms down by the side. Beginning just below the collar bone, on the center line of the body (sternum), apply LIGHT pressure from the center line outward to the inside of the shoulder joint three times each. (Photo 13) Move downward on the chest cavity and repeat the procedure. Depending on the size of the person, this outward massage using just the thumbs should continue to about the center of the pectoral muscles of the chest. Move the thumbs downward and, beginning below the line of the nipples, massage gently outward till reaching the bottom of the rib cage. One might also use one thumb and very gently apply pressure on the center line (sternum) from the top of the rib cage downward to the lower part of the rib cage. DO NOT USE FORCE ON THESE POINTS.

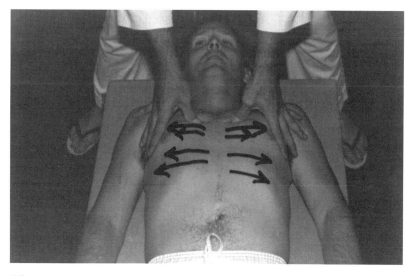

13

(7) The Neck and Shoulders

These are the last two areas and should now be worked after the person receiving the treatment is quite relaxed. NOTE: Pressure on the neck should always be gentle and not hard. (Photo 14) Use the thumb downward on the three meridians of the neck from the top to the bottom (neck root) three times each. Repeat on the opposite side of the neck. Help relax the neck by doing a gentle kneading of the neck muscles by squeezing the thumb and four fingers. By rotating the neck slowly in a circular motion and side to side, it will help to relieve any stiffness the person may have. (Photo 15) When moving the shoulders, begin by applying pressure with the thumbs at the center of the upper shoulders and moving outward three times. Then move to the top of the shoulders, using the thumbs, and beginning at the base of the neck/shoulder connection, move outward pressing down firmly to the tips of the shoulders three times. This can then be finished with a loose finger slapping massage or tapping. (Photo 16)

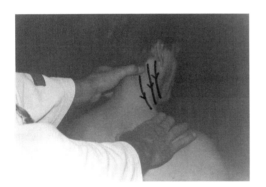

14

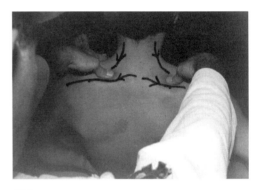

15

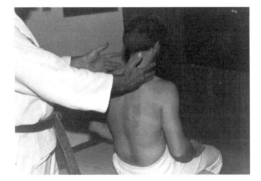

16

This entire treatment should take only about twenty minutes, yet will provide the recipient with a very relaxing and stimulating experience. It is especially welcome after a strenuous workout when many major muscles have been severely worked and definitely prevents the buildup of lactic acid in the muscles which causes much pain following a hard work out.

For more information, questions, seminars, or training please contact Mr. Palumbo by writing to:

HAKKORYU MARTIAL ARTS FEDERATION
3005 D. South Peoria Street
Aurora, CO 80014

Thanks To:

Joanna Steffen	*Photography*
Larry Royston, Bob Lucas	*Kake's*
Michael Dolce	*Book Design*
Dave Fox	*Shiatsu*

Other books by Dennis G. Palumbo
Kaiden Shihan San Dai Kichu:

The Secrets of Hakkoryu Jujutsu: Shodan Tactics

Secret Nidan Techniques of Hakkoryu Jujutsu